MW00633235

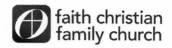

ALSO BY TERRY LEE ROBERTS

The Healthy Christian Life

Coming Soon: Heaven

From Jerusalem to Rome

How a Local Church

Can Impact the Whole World

Terry Lee Roberts

All Scripture references are from *The Holy Bible, New Living Translation*. 2nd edition. Wheaton, Illinois: Tyndale House, 2004 unless otherwise noted.

Scriptures marked NKJV are from *The New King James Version*. (1982). Nashville: Thomas Nelson.

Scriptures marked NIV are from *The Holy Bible: New International Version*. (1984). Grand Rapids, MI: Zondervan.

From Jerusalem to Rome
How a Local Church Can Impact the Whole World
ISBN 978-0-9909488-2-7

Copyright © 2016 by Terry Roberts

Faith Christian Family Church
P.O. Box 116
Warrenton, Missouri 63383

Cover photo by Tonefotografia

Printed in the United States of America

First Printing: December, 2016

www.fcfc.tv

"Only ask, and I will give you the nations as your inheritance; the whole earth as your possession."

Psalm 2:8

ACKNOWLEDGMENTS

THIS BOOK, LIKE MY MINISTRY, owes a great deal to my wife Becky. She has been an encouragement and support to me that only eternity will fully reveal. I would also like to thank Dr. Howard Foltz for his input and his role as a mentor in my life. Bill Alderman was a great help from the conception of this book to its final publication. Rory Bergman faithfully edited my many mistakes and made me sound better. A special thanks to all of the staff and the church at Faith Christian Family Church for allowing me to follow my passion.

CONTENTS

FROM JERUSALEM TO ROME

FOREWORD

LET'S TAKE A JOURNEY FROM JERUSALEM TO ROME

I INVITE YOU, ACTUALLY URGE YOU, to take a journey with the Apostle Paul and my dear friend Pastor Terry Roberts. Terry's latest book (He has written two others *The Healthy Christian Life* and *Coming Soon: Heaven) From Jerusalem to Rome* is an outstanding work that takes his experience and vision even further. This is a book of *journeys*. All of us should be on this journey's road, for it comes from the very last words of our Lord;

> *"But you will receive power when the Holy Spirit comes upon you. And you will be my witnesses, telling people about me everywhere - in Jerusalem, throughout Judea, in Samaria, and to the ends of the earth."*
> Acts 1:8 NLT.

The last words of anyone before their departure to heaven are the most important words they would speak. Terry's book will enable you to take direction from the Bible to applying practical steps in your life in a personal journey from Jerusalem to the uttermost.

My wife Pat and I have been missionaries for over 53 years. It has been my joy to preach in thousands of churches around the world. Regrettably, I frequently meet pastors in churches that do not understand how to apply the last words of Jesus to their church action plan. Some churches have no cross-cultural missions application at all, for they are singularly focused on building their own church. Emil Brunner, a Swiss theologian, said, *"As fire is to burning, so missions is to the church."* What a tragic predicament – trying to have spiritual fire without the application of Jesus last words to take the gospel to the ends of the earth.

One of the chapters of this book is entitled *Jumping Fences and Breaking Barriers*. Terry already had a heart that was on fire for missions, but he had to learn to jump some fences in applying new Biblical applications, and break some barriers of old paradigms that were hindering his church from being a healthy Great Commission church. As you read this book, you might be challenged to jump some fences and break some barriers yourself. No problem – on the other side of the fence and through the barriers is where the real global harvest emerges.

It all starts with prayer and strategic intercession. It is amazing to me how many churches only pray for their own Jerusalem and Judea. Many do not even know the names of one or two unreached people groups around the world. Terry talks about people groups, which is God's target on the ground of contemporary geography. "For God so loved the *world*," means that we should not have church just for the sake of our church, our church should be for the world. Let's love the world

Jesus died for! So Terry quotes Patrick Johnson, the original author of *Operation World*: "When we work and don't pray, we work; when we *work and pray*, God works!"

This book will help you identify your personal role and the role of your church in a focus on finishing the Great Commission. If every pastor and church would do what Terry describes in this wonderful book, that is mobilize for strategic missions and engage in the final harvest of reaching some of the 6,500 unreached people groups on God's planet - think of it - we could finish the Great Commission in our lifetime. We have 1,000 churches for every unreached people group, so we can see that finishing the Great Commission is a do-able task. The challenge is to apply the principles Terry brings out in this book.

So prayer is the front door, Biblical and strategic obedience is the pathway, and God's power is the means. You'll be blessed to read Terry's section on the power of the Holy Spirit. Terry and I have traveled together to different parts of the world and witnessed God's power at work. Thank God that He promised the power of the Holy Spirit for us to be engaged in taking the gospel to the uttermost. Otherwise, we would be helpless to fulfill the Great Commission.

So actually this is an urgent appeal from the Lord of Harvest for every Christian leader, individual believer, and church to make a commitment to the journey of Acts 1:8, Jerusalem, Judea, Samaria and to the uttermost. It is horrible to think of 47,000 people that die every day without knowing a single Christian. *THIS MUST CHANGE!* And the change starts with each believer and Christian leader to mobilize themselves, their church, and ministry.

The book's final appeal is "let's hasten the day."

"Looking for and hastening the coming of the day of God, because of which the heavens will be dissolved, being on fire, and the elements will melt with fervent heat."
2 Peter 3:12 NKJV

As we live in holy and Godly conduct each day, like Jesus who came to seek and save the lost, we can actually hasten the day of the return of our Lord and Savior. What a journey!

Howard Foltz
President AIMS

INTRODUCTION

THE BOOK OF ACTS is a great story of the early church Jesus started and left in the tiny nation of Israel. He left this unlikely group of disciples with the enormous task of spreading what they knew about Jesus and their experience with him to the entire world. They were successful and not only reached their world, but generations into the future. Approximately 2000 years after he returned to heaven, the church exists in places like South America, Asia, and the remotest islands of the earth. In John 17:20, Jesus prayed: *"I am praying not only for these disciples, but also for all who will ever believe in me through their message."* It worked!

How did they do it? In order to understand how this message reached so far, you have to see the book of Acts not just as a history of the early church, but also as a strategy and a pattern.

Jesus Christ is *Lord of the Harvest.* He directed the spread of the gospel by the Holy Spirit even when the early church wasn't sure what to do next. It is very important to see your task as a partnership with God himself, not just a human plan and effort. God is very strategic and he has a plan to get his love to every nation, tribe, and tongue. Sometimes the disciples seemed to just be reacting to persecution or circumstances. They were reacting, but God was actively overseeing and administrating the expansion of his Kingdom even through crisis and persecution. God has the final word.

Even though the disciples may not have understood what was happening and how it was happening, their actions leave us with a strategy and method to follow their example.

They continued to move into the territories laid out by Jesus in Acts 1:8:

But you will receive power when the Holy Spirit comes upon you. And you will be my witnesses, telling people about me everywhere—in Jerusalem, throughout Judea, in Samaria, and to the ends of the earth.

Our tendency is much like those of the church in Jerusalem: to sit still and enjoy the blessing of God on us, our families, and friends. In contrast, God sees the church as a movement constantly searching for new ways and new places in which to expand. The story of the book of Acts is a story of movement and expansion. It is a great history, but it also lays out a great strategy to reach our world in the 21st Century with the love of God and the powerful message of his Word.

The purpose of this book is to help you and your local church submit to the *Lord of the Harvest*, identify your areas of harvest, and engage those areas actively from where you are. Regardless of where you live on the earth, you can see the world from there.

As the pastor of a local church in a small rural town, it was easy to feel left out of the important things in the Kingdom of God. That is a false belief and the enemy has used it to paralyze a large part of the Body of Christ. When we raise our expectations, shake our faith, and move towards the goal of reaching the world, amazing things can happen. Eternity can be different if we follow God's plan instead of yielding to the lie that our efforts don't matter. They do. You and your local church are there on purpose and on time.

Before I became the pastor of a local church, I served on the mission field. Many times my wife and I sought the counsel of older and wiser ministers about whether the mission field would be a wiser use of our lives. We were advised to concentrate on mobilizing a local church to reach out rather than go overseas. That is certainly not true for everyone; the world still needs missionaries. It is also just as true that the world needs thousands of fully mobilized local churches with a heart for all the areas of the world Jesus cares about and died for.

God has a plan to actively engage his church in the mission he cares so deeply about. You have a part to play. Your local church has a calling and a unique contribution to make. It certainly includes the area where your local church is located (your Jerusalem), but it includes areas beyond that as well. The field is not just the neighborhood but the world.

Our finish line is laid out in Revelation 5:9-10:

And they sang a new song with these words: "You are worthy to take the scroll and break its seals and open it. For you were slaughtered, and your blood has ransomed people for God from every tribe and language and people and nation. And you have caused them to become a Kingdom of priests for our God. And they will reign on the earth.

PART ONE

HOW DID THE EARLY CHURCH REACH THEIR WORLD IN THE 1ST CENTURY?

CHAPTER ONE

THE BOOK OF ACTS AS A HISTORY OF GOD'S MISSION

S OMEONE HAS CORRECTLY SAID, "History, rightly interpreted, is really *His story.*" All relevant history reveals the story of the working of God among men to further his message and his kingdom. The book of Acts is no exception. It tells of a very exciting time when the church was born in the first century in Jerusalem. The early church in its infancy and with all of its shortcomings followed the example of Jesus and the power of the Holy Spirit to the best of their ability. Fortunately, someone much wiser than they was directing the church and its expansion to the nations of the world. Jesus is still *Lord of the Harvest*, and the Holy Spirit is administrating and overseeing it.

Students of the Bible have used various ways to historically understand the book of Acts. A common way is to divide it between Peter's ministry (chapters 1-12) and Paul's ministry (chapters 13-28). Peter Wagner gives another approach:

"… three broad cultural groups are highlighted in Acts 1:8: Jews, Samaritans and Gentiles. From this perspective, the entire book of Acts can be outlined around three groups:

Part I deals with church growth in Jerusalem and Judea. Evangelism is directed mostly at the Jews, and Peter is the central figure. This covers Acts 1-6.

Part II deals with church growth in Samaria. Stephen and Philip are the central figures. Stephen being the theoretician and Philip the practicioner. This covers Acts 6-8.

Part III deals with church growth among the Gentiles. Paul becomes the central figure, and this is by far Luke's largest emphasis, covering Acts 9-28, or more than two-thirds of the book. To lead in, Luke introduces Paul (Acts 9), tells how Peter blazed the trail to Cornelius's house (Acts 9-11), transitions from Peter to Paul (Acts 11-12) and then spotlights Paul's ministry for the rest of the book (Acts 13-28)." [1]

Another common division is to use Acts 1:8 as an outline for the rest of the book:

But you will receive power when the Holy Spirit comes upon you. And you will be my witnesses, telling people about me everywhere—in Jerusalem (chapters 1-7), **throughout Judea, in Samaria** (chapters 8-10), **and to the ends of the earth** (chapters 11-28).

Author John Mauck makes the argument that the book of Acts was written as a legal brief in defense of Paul's upcoming trial in Rome. *(Paul on Trial: the Book of Acts as a Defense of Christianity, Published by Thomas Nelson, 2001.)* In that case Luke would have probably gathered eyewitness accounts from believers in Jerusalem during Paul's two year imprisonment in Caesarea before he was sent to Rome for trial. That sounds like a fascinating theory, but it is just that, a theory.

A helpful, and probably the best way to understand Acts is to see it as a movement. *God started a movement in the early church that continues to this day.*

"As you read (the book of Acts,) notice the brief summary statements in 6:7; 9:31; 12:24; 16:4; and 19:20. In each case the narrative seems to pause for a moment before it takes off in a new direction of some kind. On the basis of this clue, Acts can be seen to be composed of six sections, or panels, which give the narrative a continually forward movement from its Jewish setting based in Jerusalem with Peter as its leading figure, toward a predominately Gentile church with Paul as the leading figure, and with Rome, the capital of the Gentile world, as the goal."[2]

The book of Acts describes movement. It shows the movement across geographical and cultural barriers. The Holy Spirit is seen directing and orchestrating this movement and the spread of the message. The early church was located within one nation, Israel, and composed of one type of people or people group, Jews.

"Very simply, in His last recorded words spoken on this earth, Jesus highlights two themes; power ministries and missiology"[3]

The missiology or spread of the message is a result of power encounters. The ministry of Jesus continued in his church and the result was movement. In Acts 1 Luke made an intentional connection between the ministry of Jesus as recorded in the gospel of Luke, and the ministry of Jesus as recorded in the book of Acts.

In my first book I told you, Theophilus, about everything Jesus began to do and teach until the day he was taken up to heaven after giving his chosen apostles further instructions through the Holy Spirit.

Acts 1:1-2

What Jesus began in person he continued though the Holy Spirit in the early church. He is still continuing through the modern church as we cooperate with the *Lord of the Harvest.* The greatest miracles seem to be directly connected to the movement of the message from one people group to a new one: Acts 2-Jews, Acts 8-Samaritans, and Acts 10-Gentiles as well as other examples. We need to understand these cultural bridges and utilize them in our contemporary ministry strategies.

Peter began to see a glimpse of the master plan in Acts 10 at the house of a Roman Centurion, as the Holy Spirit was poured out on the Gentiles as he had been poured out previously upon the Jews in Jerusalem. The early church wasn't sure what to do with non-Jews who wanted to be believers. A council was held in Jerusalem to settle God's will in the matter. Peter explained his actions and what had previously happened among the Gentiles at Cornelius' household to the council in Acts 15:7-11:

At the meeting, after a long discussion, Peter stood and addressed them as follows: "Brothers, you all know that God chose me from among you some time ago to preach to the Gentiles so that they could hear the Good News and believe. God knows people's hearts, and he confirmed that he accepts Gentiles by giving them the Holy Spirit, just as he did to us. He made no distinction between us and them, for he cleansed their hearts through faith. So why are you now challenging God by burdening the Gentile believers with a yoke that neither we nor our ancestors were able to bear? We believe that we are all saved the same way, by the undeserved grace of the Lord Jesus.

The leaders of the Jerusalem church wisely recognized that God intended to go beyond the Jews to get the message of the grace of God to all nations and people groups. It is commendable that they could lay aside prejudice and follow God wherever he was leading.

One of the first heresies Paul had to deal with in the early churches he planted was grace versus keeping the law. Jewish believers had grown up keeping the festivals and Sabbaths as well as being circumcised. It was understandable why they would think the first step toward Jesus would have to go through the law. Paul addressed the error that Jewish believers were somehow superior to Gentile believers in the book of Galatians. The Galatian church had added the law to the grace of God. You can almost hear Paul screaming as he tells them to stop listening to those who were trying to nullify the gospel and grace of Jesus Christ.

It was a big step for the early church to accept Gentile believers. All of their lives they had been taught the superiority of Judaism; now they were being told that in Christ, being a Jew wasn't an advantage. Of course they stumbled over the gospel of grace. Paul says that some never made it over that stumbling block. Romans 10:1-4 says;

"Brothers and sisters, my heart's desire and prayer to God on behalf of my fellow Israelites is for their salvation. For I can testify that they are zealous for God, but their zeal is

not in line with the truth. For ignoring the righteousness that comes from God, and seeking instead to establish their own righteousness, they did not submit to God's righteousness. For Christ is the end of the law, with the result that there is righteousness for everyone who believes."

In Acts 13 we see Paul, Barnabas, and others praying and fasting before the Lord. In that context the Holy Spirit spoke to release Paul and Barnabas to spread the message. They were sent out from the church at Antioch to preach the message wherever they could. The remainder of the book of Acts is the story of how that message made its way through cultures and geographical boundaries all the way to Rome. To the Jews, Rome represented *the ends of the earth.* The book of Acts ends with Paul having a ministry in Rome, and even some of Caesar's household being led to faith in Jesus Christ.

The book of Acts is a history, but also a strategy. In it God gives us the pattern for taking the message from local churches to the uttermost parts of the earth.

CHAPTER TWO

THE REAL PURPOSE OF PENTECOST

JESUS SPENT FORTY DAYS with his disciples after his resurrection. He taught them about the Kingdom of God. I wish I had the notes or a recording from those teachings. As they gathered together, Jesus spoke his last words on earth to them. Your last words are the ones you consider most important.

> *During the forty days after he suffered and died, he appeared to the apostles from time to time, and he proved to them in many ways that he was actually alive. And he talked to them about the Kingdom of God.*

> *Once when he was eating with them, he commanded them, "Do not leave Jerusalem until the Father sends you the gift he promised, as I told you before. John baptized*

with water, but in just a few days you will be baptized with the Holy Spirit."

So when the apostles were with Jesus, they kept asking him, "Lord, has the time come for you to free Israel and restore our kingdom?"

He replied, "The Father alone has the authority to set those dates and times, and they are not for you to know. But you will receive power when the Holy Spirit comes upon you. And you will be my witnesses, telling people about me everywhere—in Jerusalem, throughout Judea, in Samaria, and to the ends of the earth."

After saying this, he was taken up into a cloud while they were watching, and they could no longer see him. As they strained to see him rising into heaven, two white-robed men suddenly stood among them. "Men of Galilee," they said, "why are you standing here staring into heaven? Jesus has been taken from you into heaven, but someday he will return from heaven in the same way you saw him go!"

Acts 1:3-11

The feast of Pentecost, fifty days after Jesus was resurrected, was a very important feast for the Jews. It was one of the three times they were to appear before the Lord in Jerusalem. There were many Jews from all over the Mediterranean nations celebrating the Jewish festival of Shavu'ot, also known as the Festival of Weeks. It commemorates the first fruits of the agricultural crops being offered to the Lord. It was also a celebration of the giving of the Ten Commandments on Mount Sinai.

The festival begins on the fiftieth day after Passover. It was called Pentecost by the Greek speaking Jews because it literally means fiftieth. The feast of Pentcost is foremost a feast of *harvest*.

Jesus spent forty days with his disciples then ascended to heaven after saying they would be filled with the Holy Spirit soon. That happened ten days later on the day of Pentecost. God chose this day when the Jews from other nations would hear and witness the wonders of God.

The Holman New Testament Commentary says this about the various people groups present:

> *"Luke's list of fifteen geographical locations was a group of nations or areas in which known Jewish populations existed and would likely have sent representative groups to the Feast of Pentecost. Everyone there who spoke a language other than Greek or Aramaic heard the message of the Christians in that language-maybe fifteen languages, maybe fifty, maybe more. The languages differed; the message remained the same: the wonders of God."* [4]

God was very strategically reaching out to the Jewish people group with the gospel. The message is to the Jew first and then the Gentiles. Jesus was very clear that his first priority was to reach the Jewish people group. He had been sent in his earthly ministry to *the lost sheep of the house of Israel.* The incredible thing was that they realized God *spoke their language.*

The IVP New Testament Commentary says this about the various languages in Acts 2:

"This multilingual witness coheres with the universal offer of salvation in the church's message and its consequent worldwide mission. It also highlights the church's multicultural character. God affirms people as cultural beings. As many a Bible translator knows, our native language and culture is natural, necessary and welcome to us as the air we breathe. No wonder that when persons receive a Scripture portion in their own language they rejoice: "God speaks my language!"" [5]

God recognizes the place of people groups beginning with the Jewish people group. He said in the Great Commission Scripture in Matthew 28:18-20:

Jesus came and told his disciples, "I have been given all authority in heaven and on earth. Therefore, go and make disciples of all the nations, baptizing them in the name of the Father and the Son and the Holy Spirit. Teach these new disciples to obey all the commands I have given you. And be sure of this: I am with you always, even to the end of the age."

The Greek word for nations is *ethné*. It is used to describe nations or people groups. We recognize different ethnic groups. God does as well, and celebrates them.

Pentecost represented the first fruits. In this case it was the Jews. After the first fruits God planned a harvest among all peoples. The long-range plan of God that extended beyond Israel was revealed to Abraham much earlier when God called him.

"I will make you into a great nation. I will bless you and make you famous, and you will be a blessing to others. I will bless those who bless you and curse those who treat you with contempt. All the families on earth will be blessed through you."
Genesis 12:2-3

The Hebrew word for families is *mishpachah*. It describes nations, tribes and clans. God intended to bless Abraham's physical family, and then use it to bless all the families and tribes and clans on earth. His plan has always been to reach everyone, everywhere.

God was revealing and acting on his plan to reach all nations. Jesus' disciples, even after being with him for three years of ministry and forty days of intensive instruction after his resurrection, still didn't see the big picture. Like most of us, they were culturally centric. The Jewish culture was very closed and self-focused. In Acts 1:6, the disciples asked if this was when God would restore the physical kingdom to Israel.

So when the apostles were with Jesus, they kept asking him, "Lord, has the time come for you to free Israel and restore our kingdom?"

The full extent of their vision was to see Israel restored and blessed. Jesus made it clear that God's vision was much bigger than just Israel; it encompassed the entire world.

"But you will receive power when the Holy Spirit comes upon you. And you will be my witnesses, telling people

about me everywhere—in Jerusalem, throughout Judea, in
Samaria, and to the ends of the earth."
Acts 1:8

Jesus was expanding their vision to the entire earth. Many
Christians have the same inward focus as these disciples of Jesus. It is
natural to be self-absorbed with your culture and people group. Jesus
was saying that the purpose of Pentecost, the purpose of the infilling of
the Holy Spirit, was to motivate and empower us to reach everyone,
everywhere with the message. Christians are uniquely empowered by
God himself to carry out the promises given to Abraham and the
disciples.

A pastor's wife once said to my wife in conversation, "Our church
doesn't have a call to missions; just to our city." My first thought when I
heard that was, "I wonder if she reads the Bible?" Jesus made it clear
that everyone has a responsibility to get this message out everywhere.
You may not have a call to go personally but you are called to be
involved at some level. We can all pray, give money, and send others.

The argument of that pastor's wife is the argument of people all
over the world who are focused on just their neighborhood, city, or
nation. The reasoning is, *there are so many lost people without Jesus in my city.*
When all of them have heard and responded, then I can think about those beyond.
The problem with that thinking is revealed in Jesus' words in Acts 1:8:

"But you shall receive power when the Holy Spirit has
come upon you; and you shall be witnesses to Me in
Jerusalem, and in all Judea and Samaria, and to the end of
the earth." NKJV

Jesus didn't say Jerusalem *then* Judea *then* Samaria *then* the ends of the earth. He said Jerusalem *and* Judea *and* Samaria *and* the ends of the earth. The commission for the church is to have an outreach that is simultaneous rather than linear or sequential. The Christian church has a four-pronged call to outreach or mission.

Jesus was very clear to his disciples that they not try and figure out every detail of end-time events, but rather to focus on the task at hand. He was warning them as well as us to not lose focus. James 5:7 makes it clear what God's focus is:

See how the farmer waits for the precious fruit of the earth, waiting patiently for it until it receives the early and latter rain. NIV

The harvest of the earth is the people who will say yes to Jesus Christ when they hear the good news. The only thing that is keeping Jesus from returning is the unfinished harvest. He made very clear what must happen before his return:

And the Good News about the Kingdom will be preached throughout the whole world, so that all nations will hear it; and then the end will come.
Matthew 24:14

The word for nations is the Greek word *ethné* again. God is definitely focused on the ethnic people groups of the world and he wants us to be as well.

It is important to note from an honest Biblical interpretation that the message of Jesus, like his ministry in the gospels, spread always with power encounters. Healings, miracles, and spiritual gifts were essential to the spread of the message. Notice in Acts 8:4-8 the miracles in the church in Jerusalem that continued with Philip in Samaria:

> *Those who had been scattered preached the word wherever they went. Philip went down to a city in Samaria and proclaimed the Christ there. When the crowds heard Philip and saw the miraculous signs he did, they all paid close attention to what he said. With shrieks, evil spirits came out of many, and many paralytics and cripples were healed. So there was great joy in that city.* NIV

Paul's ministry was peppered with similar miracles and signs as well. There is no indication from Scripture that God intended to *disarm* our generation of the very tools the early church used to shake the world. Hebrews 2:3-4 says:

> *This salvation, which was first announced by the Lord, was confirmed to us by those who heard him. God also testified to it by signs, wonders and various miracles, and gifts of the Holy Spirit distributed according to his will.* NIV

The same power that was available then is available now because God doesn't change. The teaching of cessation (that gifts and miracles were only part of an apostolic age) has neutered the modern church of their ability to command the attention of a world full of skeptics and cynics.

The power of God worked most effectively and often in Scripture when barriers were being crossed and new pockets of people were being reached. Miracles in the book of Acts were primarily connected to *movement.* That same power that started on the Day of Pentecost is accessible to those who follow the command and commission of Jesus. The purpose of Pentecost was to empower Jesus' followers to reach the world and crash through all opposition to the message.

CHAPTER THREE

JUMPING FENCES AND BREAKING BARRIERS

REMEMBER THE KEY PHRASE in the book of Acts is *movement*. By human nature people tend to settle and focus on where they are now. The Holy Spirit was orchestrating a movement that was focused on the ends of the earth and everything in between.

In Acts 1:8 Jesus issued the call to "keep moving" until all of the earth was reached. Things were going so well in Jerusalem that the disciples became content to just enjoy the blessings and growth. If we aren't obedient to do Acts 1:8 we often invite an event like happened in Acts 8:1

A great wave of persecution began that day, sweeping over the church in Jerusalem; and all the believers except the apostles were scattered through the regions of Judea and Samaria.

Because they didn't go obediently to preach; they were scattered to preach. The original call to reach Judea and Samaria had to be implemented by persecution. History has many examples of people with the knowledge of God staying put until events occurred to compel them to do what they were commanded to do. As one Bible commentary said:

> *"Now the Christians were forced to do what they had been reluctant to do – get the message of Jesus out to the surrounding* **regions**. *... there are two different words in the ancient Greek language for the idea of "scattered." One has the idea of scattering in the sense of making something disappear, like scattering someone's ashes. The other word has the idea of scattering in the sense of planting or sowing seeds. This is the ancient Greek word used here. In Acts 1:8, Jesus clearly told His followers to look beyond Jerusalem and bring the gospel to Judea, Samaria, and the whole world. But to this point, Jesus' followers had not done this.*

> *The resulting good of the spread of the gospel leads some to see this persecution as being the will of God. God can and will use pressing circumstances to guide us into His will. Sometimes we have to be shaken out of our comfortable state before we do what God wants us to do."* [5]

The intention of Jesus was for the message to continue in *ever widening circles*. Paul makes reference to this idea in his second letter to the Corinthians:

> **Nor do we boast and claim credit for the work someone else has done. Instead, we hope that your faith will grow so that <u>the boundaries of our work among you will be extended</u>. Then we will be able to go and preach the Good News in other places far beyond you, where no one else is working.** 2 Corinthians 10:15-16

The New International Version says it this way:

Our hope is that, as your faith continues to grow, our <u>area</u> <u>of activity among you will greatly expand</u>, so that we can preach the gospel in the regions beyond you.

There again is the idea of *movement*. This expansion requires that boundaries be broken through. The church in Acts was completely Jewish in the beginning. They had to jump over cultural and language barriers to the Gentiles. Remember the church council in Acts 15 where it was decided that God wants to break cultural and religious barriers to present truth to all people.

Many barriers exist: from language, to geographical boundaries, to deep seated differences in worldviews. Those who study missions have identified these barriers as E-0 to E-3 barriers. This method is called the *E-Scale. E* stands for evangelism, and the number represents how many barriers have to be crossed in order to share the message of Jesus with a listener.

E-0 represents those *in the church* who have never been converted. They simply attend church, but don't have a personal relationship with God. No cultural barriers have to be crossed in order to reach them.

E-1 represents evangelism that is from the church *to the community*. This is outreach to near neighbors with whom you share a culture. Even though they are not currently part of the church community, they are part of the larger community. These people are potential future Christians. The barrier in this case is the message itself. The message is an offense to those who don't see what Jesus did as relevant to them.

E-2 represents those who have a *different culture* than you. In addition to the barrier from the church to the community, you also have cultural and usually language barriers. You have to jump at least two fences to get to these folks. This type of evangelism may be aimed at immigrant communities that have moved to your area. This issue isn't so much the geographical distance between you, but the barriers that you must be aware of and strategically overcome. E-2 represents *Samaria*.

E-3 evangelism is to the *uttermost parts of the earth*. Here, those who need to be reached in this world think, act, and speak differently than you. They are often a far distance away as well, even though it is possible to have these people nearby geographically as refugees. Whether geographically close or on the other side of the world, this involves reaching people far away from your culture. It requires jumping over three fences: the church to the community barrier, the cultural/language barrier, and a *radically different* cultural/geographic barrier. This type is the most difficult but everyone should be involved in it in some measure. This may be praying for and supporting those laboring in the 10/40 Window without ever going there yourself.

It is a helpful exercise to ask yourself, "What is stopping me?" What is standing between you and your church having a world-class missions outreach to all four target areas mentioned by Jesus?

Every barrier presented a problem to the early church, but with the leadership of the Holy Spirit they crashed through them in order to rescue those on the other side of those fences and barriers.

The primary barriers faced by the early church are the same as those faced by the contemporary church. Conquered barriers become gateways to new territory. Here are the obvious barriers faced by the early church as well as the modern church in addition to the barriers mentioned above of the message, the culture, language, and geography.

BARRIER 1 - AN UNCLEAR OR FAULTY INTERPRETATION OF SCRIPTURE AND THE PURPOSE OF GOD

Many Bible schools and seminaries do not offer courses in reaching the world. Pastors are taught often to reach only their Jerusalem (local areas). Christians who read the Great Commission of Jesus to the church think only in terms of their near neighbors and exclude the unreached. The Apostolic call on the Apostle Paul and the early church was to *ever-widening circles of influence.*

> **Nor do we boast and claim credit for the work someone else has done. Instead, we hope that your faith will grow so that the boundaries of our work among you will be extended. Then we will be able to go and preach the Good News in other places far beyond you, where no one else is working**
>
> 2 Corinthians 10:15-16

Not everyone in the early church understood what God was planning. Peter was shown in a vision that God wanted to reach beyond the Jews. It was still an issue in Acts 15 when the church met to decide what to do with the Gentiles who wanted to follow Jesus.

BARRIER 2 - FEAR OF OTHER CULTURES AND PEOPLE GROUPS (XENOPHOBIA)

The early church was almost entirely Jewish, and as Jews they had been taught for centuries to steer clear of the Gentiles. It was a dramatic experience when God showed Peter the sheet let down from heaven in Acts 10. The sheet was filled with non-kosher foods representing the Gentiles. God was breaking down the barrier between people groups so his love could reach to non-Jews as well. The Jewish early church also struggled with the Samaritans who were half Jewish and half Gentile. The cultural barrier was a fence that seemed very difficult to jump over. We face those same fences between cultures in contemporary societies. Like Jonah in Nineveh, we have people groups that we don't naturally want to reach out to. Remember, God so loved *the world* that he sent Jesus.

BARRIER 3 - SPIRITUAL WARFARE

The enemy, Satan, wants to keep people from the message of Jesus Christ so he acts to hinder those who preach the good news. Prayer and the believer knowing his authority in prayer are vital to getting the message to ever widening circles. In 2 Corinthians 10, Paul says the area of influence increases as your faith increases. It is directly related to what you believe and how you pray.

Jesus said in order to reach into darkness two things are needed, prayer and movement. He said in Matthew 12:29:

For who is powerful enough to enter the house of a strong man like Satan and plunder his goods? Only someone even stronger—someone who could tie him up and then plunder his house.

Notice that you must first tie up the enemy. One translation says *bind the strongman.*

After praying with authority...move. Intentionally take action to reach those who are in bondage and slavery to Satan. Clear out the jailhouse and set the prisoners free! Christians and churches have often done one or the other. Both are needed to *rob his house.*

A final word: Be strong in the Lord and in his mighty power. Put on all of God's armor so that you will be able to stand firm against all strategies of the devil. For we are not fighting against flesh-and-blood enemies, but against evil rulers and authorities of the unseen world, against mighty powers in this dark world, and against evil spirits in the heavenly places.
Ephesians 6:10-12

In 1987 Ronald Reagan stood at the Brandenburg Gate in Berlin. He told Mr. Gorbachev to *"tear down this wall."* He was speaking about the Iron Curtain that kept people in Eastern Europe in slavery to communism. We can have the same approach to Satan who has kept over three billion people behind the wall of exclusion from the gospel. Our message is: *Satan, tear down this wall!*

CHAPTER FOUR

REACHING NEW PEOPLE GROUPS

THE BOOK OF ACTS DETAILS the spread of the gospel to new people groups by the direction of the Holy Spirit. On the Day of Pentecost the people group was primarily Jewish. Their culture, their language, and their belief system were totally Jewish even though they represented different geopolitical nations.

From their history and covenant with God, Jews knew they were the chosen people. Over time it became more and more about them and less and less about others. God's intention was to use Israel as a blessing and light to the nations. The message got stuck when their focus got stuck.

That self-absorption was still evident in Acts 1 when the disciples asked Jesus if this was the time to restore the kingdom to Israel. They were still under the impression that the plan of God was only about them and their nation. Many churches have the same issue facing them. Our focus can become more us and less them.

Jesus' response in Acts 1 was to tell them to get their eyes off of themselves and spread the message to everyone. It should give us hope to know that after being physically present with Jesus for over three years, they had lost focus. The Holy Spirit is sent to restore and recharge our focus to *the harvest*.

The early Christian church was so Jewish that for a time it was viewed as simply a sect within Judaism. Only after various encounters with Gentiles who wanted to follow Jesus, did the Jewish church have to decide where new people groups fit within the wider church. It wasn't well received by all Jewish believers that Gentiles could have equal status with believing Jews. We see this controversy played out in Paul's travels as well as back in Jerusalem.

The Hellenist (Greek speaking) Jews had an internal church controversy with the Hebrew speaking Jews over the feeding of widows. This conflict was skillfully handled by the selection and approval of seven men to handle the food distribution.

The gospel then spread to Judea and Samaria in Acts 8. The death of Stephen caused persecution of the early church. The result was that the apostles stayed in Jerusalem while the church as a whole was dispersed. They preached as they went; to everyone they encountered. What the enemy meant for evil God used to spread the message even further.

Also in Acts 8 we see the Holy Spirit orchestrate evangelism by sending Philip to an Ethiopian eunuch. The Ethiopian had traveled to

Jerusalem to worship God, but left unfulfilled. Philip was able to lead him to salvation and water baptism right on the road. The eunuch had great authority under Candace, queen of the Ethiopians, so it is probable that as he returned home he had a great influence as a follower of Jesus. History reveals that the Ethiopian church was one of the earliest Christian groups.

In Acts 10 the doors are blown wide open to the Gentiles as Peter receives a vision from the Lord. In this vision he sees non-kosher and unclean foods. God tells him to eat these foods but Peter, as a Jew, resists. The message is that whatever God calls clean, food or people, is actually clean. Of course we see that the Holy Spirit was directing Peter to take the message to Gentiles.

Events unfold to locate Peter in the house of a Roman soldier named Cornelius. Cornelius knows that Peter is coming to speak to them on behalf of God. He gathered his relatives and close friends to hear the message as well. As Peter was preaching, the Gentiles experienced a similar occurrence as the Jews in Jerusalem had experienced on Pentecost. The Holy Spirit was poured out and they began to speak in other tongues. Peter and his companions recognized this as an act of God and baptized these Gentiles into the church.

In Acts 11, we see that the new Jewish Christians in Jerusalem were not ready to agree that Peter's mission to Gentiles was acceptable. Peter defended himself and explained how the Holy Spirit had put the meeting at Cornelius' house together, and how the Holy Spirit was poured out on non-Jewish people. The church reluctantly accepted that perhaps God was concerned for people beyond the Jewish race.

"As I began to speak," Peter continued, "the Holy Spirit fell on them, just as he fell on us at the beginning. Then I thought of the Lord's words when he said, 'John baptized with water, but you will be baptized with the Holy Spirit.' And since God gave these Gentiles the same gift he gave us when we believed in the Lord Jesus Christ, who was I to stand in God's way?"

When the others heard this, they stopped objecting and began praising God. They said, "We can see that God has also given the Gentiles the privilege of repenting of their sins and receiving eternal life."

Meanwhile, the believers who had been scattered during the persecution after Stephen's death traveled as far as Phoenicia, Cyprus, and Antioch of Syria. They preached the word of God, but only to Jews. However, some of the believers who went to Antioch from Cyprus and Cyrene began preaching to the Gentiles about the Lord Jesus. The power of the Lord was with them, and a large number of these Gentiles believed and turned to the Lord.
Acts 11:15-21

We see in verse 19, that other believers had reached out beyond the Jews as well. Specifically, the believers went to Phoenicia, the Mediterranean island of Cyprus, and Antioch in Syria. It was in Antioch that the Gentile church began to gain traction. Barnabas traveled to Antioch to follow up on the reports and was glad to see the evidence of the grace of God upon the Gentiles. He located Paul and the two of them, along with other leaders, taught the church and oversaw its growth and strengthening. The believers were called *Christians* for the first time here in this city. They acknowledged their distinctness as followers of Jesus yet without being Jewish. *The gospel had successfully broken the culture, language, and geographical barriers.*

Arguably, from Antioch the first intentional missions outreach began. While the church in Jerusalem was reluctant to reach beyond its borders, the Antioch church seemed enthusiastic to reach other cultures. As the church leaders in Antioch conducted a prayer meeting and worship service to the Lord, the Holy Spirit spoke specifically about the task of going further with the message. Paul and Barnabas had undoubtedly sensed a call to go, but this prophetic word confirmed their call.

Paul and Barnabas were *sent out* from the local church. This established a precedent and pattern for all local churches. Every local church was to assume responsibility to become a sending agency as much as possible. Mission agencies and parachurch organizations have taken up the task of mission sending as the local churches around the world have refused to be sending churches. God intended for local churches to accept the mantle and call of mission sending. Thank God that churches are beginning to respond. It has been said, "The local church is the hope of the world." I would add *the whole world.*

From this point on in Acts, we see missionary journeys and intentional expansion. We see Paul and Barnabas reach out to Cyprus, and travel on to modern day Turkey. Paul makes a total of three missionary journeys as well as a final trip to Rome where he was prosecuted. Paul made it clear that he wanted to reach the Romans and even travel to Spain if that were possible.

In Acts 15, the leaders of the church met to settle once and for all if the message is indeed intended for all mankind. They overwhelmingly decided that the Gentiles were to hear the gospel and not be burdened with Jewish cultural requirements. They wrote a letter explaining their decision and it was joyfully received by the Gentile believers.

Even though we see Paul and other early Christians very motivated to spread the message, it is important to realize that the Holy Spirit was the driving force and chief strategist. An example of this is in Acts 16. Paul and his company actively try to enter certain areas to preach and the Holy Spirit redirects them.

> **Next Paul and Silas traveled through the area of Phrygia and Galatia, because the Holy Spirit had prevented them from preaching the word in the province of Asia at that time. Then coming to the borders of Mysia, they headed north for the province of Bithynia, but again the Spirit of Jesus did not allow them to go there. So instead, they went on through Mysia to the seaport of Troas.**
>
> **That night Paul had a vision: A man from Macedonia in northern Greece was standing there, pleading with him, "Come over to Macedonia and help us!" So we decided to leave for Macedonia at once, having concluded that God was calling us to preach the Good News there.**
> Acts 16:6-10

The Holy Spirit stopped them from going where they wanted to go, so they could instead be sent to the continent of Europe and plant the message in a new continent. Jesus is the *Lord of the Harvest* and the Holy Spirit is the *chief strategist*. His leadership is key to all of us playing our part and being sent to the right people, at the right time, in the right place.

The book of Acts ends with Paul being taken to Rome to stand before Caesar. Tradition says he may have been released and then imprisoned a second time before being martyred for his faith. Whether that happened or not, the book of Acts ends with Paul in Rome preaching to all who would listen. Even those in Caesar's household were impacted with the gospel.

To the Jews in Jerusalem, Rome was considered the furthest outreaches of civilization. Rome indeed represented *the uttermost* to them. They had been successful in spite of themselves in reaching their world with the message.

It is important to see the book of Acts as the history of the movement of the message but also as a strategy for a movement. The target is the same. God wants every nation and people group to hear the good news.

The method is the same as well. The movement of the message is intended to be marked by power encounters and miracles. Barriers are broken down, not by intellect but by God's power demonstrated through faithful followers of Jesus.

In Mark 16 as Jesus lays out the Great Commission, he says signs, healings, and manifestations of the Holy Spirit would follow and accompany believers. God validates his message with his signature: signs and wonders.

The key to miracles seems to be the movement of the message. As the message spreads there is a greater occurrence of power. The important thing for believers to do is *keep it moving!*

The early church had to face cultural barriers, language barriers, religious barriers, geographical barriers, and deeply held prejudice against new people groups, but they witnessed breakthroughs. By the power of the Holy Spirit and a clear vision to keep the message moving, they were able to impact their world with the message of Jesus Christ.

At the end of the Book of Acts we see Paul preaching unhindered from Rome and even some of Caesar's household have come to trust in Jesus as the Messiah. They were successful! They had gone from Jerusalem to Rome.

PART TWO

How Can We Follow the First Century Strategy in the Book of Acts to Reach Our World in The 21ST Century?

CHAPTER FIVE

OUR STORY

AT THIS WRITING my wife and I will soon be pastoring the same church for 32 years. We are in a rural Missouri town about an hour outside of St. Louis. The church has grown, and we have had a wonderful season of ministry here.

As I stated earlier, the first desire of my heart was in missions. I was an assistant pastor at a church in Glasgow, Scotland, and have made over 40 short-term missions trips. My earliest spiritual mentors instilled in me a love for missions. I understood early on that God's heart was for the entire world.

In light of that, it is interesting that Becky and I have been at this church for so long. Even though we really love the people of this church, we tried several times to stop pastoring and go overseas as missionaries. In each case the Lord seemed to tell us to stay. We sought the advice of people we trusted, and received great advice to raise up a mobilized church to focus on and support missions rather than going ourselves as missionaries.

Even though we gave a tithe of our income to missions and sent out short-term missionaries from our church, we didn't have a great strategy to finish the task of world evangelization. I noticed that other pastors and churches gave money to missions but usually it was to friends from Bible school. There is nothing wrong with the missionaries being friends, as long as the church is being strategic about reaching the world.

I returned to school at Regent University where I met my mission professor, Dr. Howard Foltz. In my courses with him he talked about having a *fully-orbed* mission program based on Acts 1:8, to our Jerusalem, Judea, Samaria, and the uttermost.

The area where we really fell short was in the area of the uttermost. The unreached areas of the world are usually the most neglected, mainly just because of oversight and lack of strategy. Most pastors don't know missionaries who are focusing on the unreached of the world. It isn't necessarily that they don't want to reach the unreached, they simply don't know how.

Our association with Dr. Foltz and the organization he started (Accelerating International Mission Strategies or AIMS), helped us reach out to the unreached in partnership by training missionaries and church planters in the unreached areas of the earth. We also began working with another ministry reaching the 10/40 window. Reaching the unreached can feel like an impossible task. Some churches may know missionaries that do it well, but to most pastors it truly is another world. The best way to begin is to find someone who is effectively reaching the unreached and partner with them. It may just be with financial support, and it may involve eventually going or sending from your church. The Holy Spirit directed us and gave us divine connections with effective missionaries, and he will do that for any church that is open to his plan for them.

Our outreach is now geared towards all four areas of outreach. It took a few years, a lot of prayer, and some experimentation. We have even made some mistakes and missteps along the way. Our church can't reach the whole world but working in partnership with others, we can do our part.

I am not usually a person who has dreams and visions, even though I believe they are thoroughly Biblical. In the first few years as pastor at this church I had a dream. After waking I was convinced that it had been a dream from the Lord. I still believe it was even though I probably misinterpreted it for quite some time.

In the dream I was in a foreign nation where a great revival was taking place. Many people were making the decision to follow Jesus. I was frustrated because I didn't have a good way to follow up with the new believers and I expressed that frustration out loud. Without seeing the Lord, or an angel, or hearing a voice, I said in the dream, "I know what I will do. I will do what they did in the Bible." With that, I followed the pattern of Jesus in Luke 9:10-17. In the story there were many hungry people and the disciples didn't know what to do. They told Jesus and he had the people get into groups of about fifty each. He blessed the food and gave it to the disciples and all were fed.

Upon waking I thought the dream was about small groups. Out of this we launched small groups in the church and they have been very successful. I now believe the subject of the dream was simple or house churches planted in a church planting movement. A church planting movement is the rapid multiplication of churches in a culture. When it happens, it is obviously a work ordered and overseen by the Lord. That is happening all over the world in many different cultures, and I believe it will increase in the coming years.

Through organizations like AIMS and others, we have been able to sponsor hundreds of native churches in the unreached parts of the world. I want to encourage other churches and pastors that your impact can be greatly multiplied if you learn to become more strategic. All missions efforts are smart, but some missions efforts are *smarter*.

CHAPTER SIX

WRITING YOUR STORY

GOD HAS A UNIQUE and specific plan and purpose for every local church. Jesus said to reach Jerusalem, Judea, Samaria, and the ends of the earth. The Holy Spirit has a plan to help you fulfill that in your unique context and setting. Every individual and every local church should have a world vision. We are called and equipped to reach each area *simultaneously* if we follow his plan.

Acts gives us not just a history of missions, but a strategy as well. By following the example and even failures of the early church, we can discover and implement God's eternal plan to bring love and truth to all men everywhere. It is very healthy to ask *how* the early church was so effective, and what we should do to discover and implement that method in the 21st century.

The heart and source of missions is designed and intended to flow out of the local church. In Acts, the church in Jerusalem and Antioch accepted responsibility to send out those called to expand the message.

In the past, para-church missions agencies have been forced to do what was originally the church's calling.

As the leadership of a local church seeks God's calling, he reveals a strategy to touch locally and internationally. God wants every church and every church leader to have faith that changes the world.

As a pastor for over three decades, I have seen some missionaries speak condescendingly to pastors who have a heart for and preach to their local community. Many times they have been told by well meaning missionaries, "No one deserves to hear the gospel twice until everyone has heard it once." It is very easy for them to leave the impression that all God cares about is the world and not the church. That is not God's heart. He loves each local church and the communities they are reaching. Missions are actually designed to be an overflow of a healthy Jerusalem (local church).

The other extreme of that message is to project that God only wants us to reach beyond ourselves after everyone in our local community has heard the Gospel. Both extremes miss the point. A healthy Jerusalem church can reach locally and internationally at the same time, if churches and missionaries work together to complement each other's ministry rather than compete.

God never desired for the local church to compete with world missions. He designed the local church to be the impetus and source of missions. The only way to effectively reach the world is to affirm the local church and local church leadership wherever it is. It is easy as a pastor to start thinking that the local church isn't appreciated by missionaries, yet should be a source of funding for what really matters. It is difficult to be in partnership with someone who only sees you as the *junior partner.* The local church and missionaries can and should work together to reach the harvest of all the earth.

Churches have prayer meetings, retreats, and brainstorming sessions to determine God's purpose for that local church. I would encourage those churches to continue that process with the world in mind. Discover not just your local purpose, but how God would use you to reach into the world as well. Just as there is a local call, every New Testament church has a call to assist in getting the message to those beyond as well. God believes in you and trusts you to *be* his heart for the world.

In the next few chapters we will begin to discuss specifically how a local church and its leadership can expand its heart to encompass God's entire vision.

CHAPTER SEVEN

SEE THE HARVEST

J ESUS TOLD HIS DISCIPLES to *see* the harvest in John 4:35,

"You know the saying, 'Four months between planting and harvest.' But I say, wake up and look around. The fields are already ripe for harvest."

The disciples were aware of the problems they faced but they didn't see the potential. Jesus was saying to wake up and become aware of the people in their world who were *ripe* to respond to the message of God's love.

James 5:7 makes it clear that the harvest is people:

Dear brothers and sisters, be patient as you wait for the Lord's return. Consider the farmers who patiently wait for the rains in the fall and in the spring. They eagerly look for the valuable harvest to ripen.

Look at the harvest. Become aware of the world in which you live. *Operation World* is a prayer manual that exposes you to the prayer needs of every country and specifically lists the prayer needs for that country or region. This is one way to understand the world around you. You can see the world from wherever you are. (Operation World 21st Century Edition by Patrick Johnstone and Jason Mandryk published in 2001 is available online.)

Often we can lose sight of the harvest potential because we hear so much from our culture that is negative and depressing. We need to intentionally seek out reports of what God is doing. Often we find them behind the scenes or underground in far-flung places around the world. Reports abound of revival behind the scenes in unlikely places like China, Iran, and other restricted access nations.

A well-known missionary evangelist said when he hears the word *refugee*, he thinks *revival*. Just as persecution and bad circumstances produced a harvest of people in places the early church had not planned, modern day persecution can be like gasoline on a fire. Isaiah 60:2-3 presents a picture of God's work accelerating during persecution and increasing world darkness:

> **Darkness as black as night covers all the nations of the earth, but the glory of the Lord rises and appears over you. All nations will come to your light; mighty kings will come to see your radiance.**

Psalm 23 tells us that God prepares a table for us *in the presence of our enemies.* God is a good steward; he will use anything and everything to accomplish his purpose.

If you don't see the harvest, you won't be inclined to reap the harvest. We all act on our perception of truth even if it is wrong. Wrong and incomplete information can cause you to not be walking in the light and the truth.

Seeing the harvest begins in your neighborhood. Learn to see the people around you like God sees them. Ask God to open your eyes to the truth about people - their hurts and problems. God will begin to release his compassion through you and it will not leave you unchanged. Once your heart is stretched towards people, it will never return to its original state.

Sometimes it is necessary to go see the harvest. A short-term mission trip gives you a perspective of real life and real people in another setting. Being there helps you see more clearly.

Expose yourself and your church to people of other cultures. You can do that in person or by watching television shows or movies about other cultures. Even a travel channel can make you see people outside of your world. There have even been people who go overseas on vacation and return with a changed heart. If you can be around other cultures and see that they are people with thoughts, feelings, needs and wants just like yours, it really opens your eyes.

Over the years our church has brought in guest speakers who were from other cultures than ours so our local body has the opportunity to get an international perspective. All Christians should be World Christians, seeing the importance of the world for which Jesus died.

I was once in another country walking along when it occurred to me, *you can see the world from here.* I thought about the fact that it is true from wherever you are on earth. You can see the world *from here.*

CHAPTER EIGHT

PRAY FOR THE HARVEST

"...for my house will be called a house of prayer for all nations." The Sovereign Lord declares— he who gathers the exiles of Israel: "I will gather still others to them besides those already gathered."
Isaiah 56:7-8 NIV

Ask of me, and I will make the nations your inheritance, the ends of the earth your possession.
Psalm 2:8 NIV

The harvest is plentiful, but the workers are few. Ask the Lord of the harvest, therefore, to send out workers into his harvest field.
Luke 10:2 NIV

J ESUS WAS VERY CLEAR about the place of prayer when it comes to reaching the harvest. He is the *Lord of the Harvest*, and he said to ask him to send laborers into the harvest.

Up until this time Jesus had been teaching, preaching, and healing the sick. His ministry multiplied when he included his disciples in ministry. Jesus was all about raising up laborers to help him tell the story and do the ministry.

Prayer is the act of binding the strongman before robbing his house. Robbing his house is receiving the harvest. Prayer and evangelism must go together to be effective. Some churches pray but never go themselves or send workers. Some may go and send but not pray first. Binding the strongman in prayer and going into the harvest are like the two blades of a pair of scissors. Both are necessary and essential to doing the job effectively.

Individuals praying, as well as corporate prayer set the stage for God to act. Someone said, "When we work, *we work*. When we pray, *God works*." The Bible clearly lays out the authority that has been given to Christians in Jesus Christ. Those who understand that authority and the power in the name of Jesus can change nations from their prayer closet. God enforces his will on the earth when his people pray.

The God of peace will soon crush Satan under your feet.
Romans 16:20

In the early days of pastoring in rural Missouri, my wife and I had an experience that shook our theology but eventually helped us reach more people. My wife Becky was sleeping and I was awake. At the exact same time, she had a dream of a demon in our house and I suddenly experienced an evil presence in my house. It was so real I couldn't speak or move. I started having fear and strange thoughts; I knew I had to deal with it spiritually. The fear was palpable.

Not knowing what to do or how to address this presence, I took my Bible into the next room and was drawn to 1 John 4:4 from the NIV:

You, dear children, are from God and have overcome them, because the one who is in you is greater than the one who is in the world.

After a few minutes, it registered in my heart and a divine authority rose up inside me. I rebuked the spiritual force and fear left. The Bible gave me the confidence I needed to conquer that spirit. Paul had told the Corinthians that as their faith increased he would be able to work among them in ever-widening circles (2 Corinthians 10:15).

That is exactly what happened in our local church. Suddenly, for no apparent reason, we began to grow and reach the lost like never before. We are convinced that the battle had been won spiritually and growth was the direct result of the enemy losing ground. We didn't go looking for a demon; Jesus never went demon hunting. On his way to help people, he encountered demons who wanted to kill, steal from, and destroy the people God loved. He dealt with them in the context of helping people.

A famous missionary from the last century had moved to the Philippines and was not being very effective. One day he heard a radio broadcast from a jail cell in Manila. A young girl who was in jail was demon possessed and was acting out in ways that frightened the police and city officials. Her demonic screams were even broadcast on the radio; fear prevailed, and no one knew what to do. The missionary went to the jail and after fasting and prayer cast the spirit out. The girl was delivered and visibly free. As a result, the missionary was given access to a large stadium where he conducted meetings and planted a large church as a result. That church is still there in Manila and decades later, has an attendance of thousands. He didn't go looking for demons, but encountering the demon with power resulted in the church being greatly expanded.

As you move further into the enemy's territory, he will show up to resist you. Don't fear, push on and destroy the work of the enemy. God will crush him as you and I move forward in faith.

CHAPTER NINE

IDENTIFY YOUR HARVEST FIELD

JESUS SENT THE CHURCH into four specific intentional areas to reap a harvest. In Acts 1:8 Jesus identifies those four areas:

> *But you will receive power when the Holy Spirit comes upon you. And you will be my witnesses, telling people about me everywhere—in <u>Jerusalem</u>, throughout <u>Judea</u>, in <u>Samaria</u>, and to the <u>ends of the earth</u>.*

The task of every church leader is to identify the four specific areas Jesus commanded us to reach.

JERUSALEM

Jerusalem was the local church where everything started. Jesus was crucified and resurrected in Jerusalem. The Holy Spirit was poured out on the church in Jerusalem. *Your Jerusalem* is your local church. It is your local community and neighborhood.

This is your first priority as a local church pastor. It has been said, "The light that shines the farthest, shines brightest at home." Your first field is your Jerusalem. As you reach the people in your Jerusalem, they have the potential to become a part of your church. This principle is true for every local church on earth regardless of size or location. If you want a greater harvest; believe God for a greater harvest in your Jerusalem. In so doing, you will have a greater base to impact other areas of harvest around the world.

It is very important to affirm the role of your Jerusalem in local outreach. This is where mission begins, and it is a step that can't be skipped. Unwittingly, those with a heart for the world have projected that this first step is finished and therefore unnecessary, especially in America where the gospel abounds. Not only is that false, it actually hinders the message going around the world. It all begins here! Local church, whether it is mega, house, simple, or any other flavor or type, is extremely important to Jesus Christ. That is what he is building on the earth. Matthew 16:18 records Jesus' perspective on this matter:

...and upon this rock I will build my church, and all the powers of hell will not conquer it.

JUDEA

Judea was made up of the southern portion of Israel including the city of Jerusalem. It was a local region as well as a city. The Judeans in southern Israel were much different from the Galileans in the north. The Galileans were the country cousins of the Judeans and having a distinct accent, were thought to be like hillbillies. They were agricultural, and probably the country folks of Israel to the Judeans.

Your Judea is the same culture as yours, but probably in a bigger area. This may be your region, your state, or even your nation. This group is very similar to you, but not likely to be close enough to be part of your Jerusalem.

We have prayerfully decided that our role in the Significant Church Network is currently our Judea. It was created to encourage and inspire churches in small county America. Most Christians in America attend these smaller churches, often in out of the way places. The pastors often feel less important than those of mega churches. God doesn't see it like that, so we want to be part of encouraging them to keep reaching and keep flourishing.

Your Judea could be a regional church planting movement, or an affiliation with an organization similar to Significant Church Network. (significantchurch.com) You may already have an outreach to your Judea. It may just be a matter of identifying and marking it. Your denomination or church network may be this Judea for you. Find it, affirm it, and support it.

SAMARIA

Who were the Samaritans of Jesus time? The answer if found in the following:

> *"The Samaritans occupied the country formerly belonging to the tribe of Ephraim and the half-tribe of Manasseh. The capital of the country was Samaria, formerly a large and splendid city. When the ten tribes were carried away into captivity to Assyria, the king of Assyria sent people from Cutha, Ava, Hamath, and Sepharvaim to inhabit Samaria (2* Kings 17:24; Ezra 4:2-11). *These foreigners intermarried with the Israelite population that was still in and around Samaria. These "Samaritans" at first worshipped the idols of their own nations, but being troubled with lions, they supposed it was because they had not honored the God of that territory. A Jewish priest was therefore sent to them from Assyria to instruct them in the Jewish religion. They were instructed from the books of Moses, but still retained many of their idolatrous customs. The Samaritans embraced a religion that was a mixture of Judaism and idolatry (2* Kings 17:26-28). *Because the Israelite inhabitants of Samaria had intermarried with the foreigners and adopted their idolatrous religion, Samaritans were generally considered "half-breeds" and were universally despised by the Jews."*[7]

Your Samaria is different cultures, whether they are nearby or across the sea. They may simply be a local immigrant community.

Just as easily they could be geographically far away in Europe or South America. Most local churches already put foreign missions money into this category because of a relationship with someone who is already working in that field.

For our church this is primarily Haiti and Europe. I served as an assistant pastor in Glasgow, Scotland and have made many trips to Eastern and Western Europe. We would love to see another reformation there, and work towards our Samaria goal by consistently supporting missionaries active in both Europe and Haiti.

Xenophobia (fear of foreign cultures), can keep us from reaching out to those we may disagree with in matters of politics and culture. Like Jonah who was sent to the Ninevites, we must learn to love the people of a culture even if that culture is different from ours. Christians and Christian churches should be exemplifying and modeling that attitude and behavior to the world around us. Jesus said we are to be salt and light to our culture. Racism and hatred have no place in our culture and especially in our churches. Martin Luther King Jr. said:

"I have decided to stick with love. Hate is too great a burden to bear."[8]

Just as you are called to your Jerusalem and Judea, you are called to your Samaria. They may have access to the gospel in their language already, and Christian workers may already be among them, but they are still one quarter of the target to which Jesus aimed us.

ENDS OF THE EARTH

The *ends of the earth* are those who have never heard the good news of the gospel, and may have never heard the name of Jesus mentioned. Currently this represents about three billion of the seven billion people on the earth. According to the Joshua Project:

"So how many of the approximately 16,300 ethnic people groups are considered unreached i.e. less than 2% Christ-follower and less than 5% Professing Christian? The latest estimates suggest that approximately 6,550 people groups are considered unreached. That means over 40% of the world's people groups have no indigenous community of believing Christians able to evangelize the rest of their people group. Over 42% of the world's population live in these over 6,550 people groups." [9]

When we think about missions, we tend to think of geographical and political borders. In Scripture, another term is used because borders of nations are always changing. Look at the changes in European borders in just the past century. The default category to focus on is *people groups.*

I will bless those who bless you and curse those who treat you with contempt. All the families on earth will be blessed through you.
Genesis 12:3

The Hebrew word for families is *mishpâchâh.* It literally means; *a family, a circle of relatives, a class of persons, a species, a tribe or a people.* [10]

And the Good News about the Kingdom will be preached throughout the whole world, so that all <u>nations</u> will hear it; and then the end will come.
Matthew 24:14

The Greek word for nations is *ethné.* It literally means *a multitude, people, race, belonging and living together.* [11] We get our word for ethnic groups from this root word. It is used again in Matthew 28 at what is known as the Great Commission:

Jesus came and told his disciples, "I have been given all authority in heaven and on earth. Therefore, go and make disciples of all the <u>nations</u>, baptizing them in the name of the Father and the Son and the Holy Spirit. Teach these new disciples to obey all the commands I have given you. And be sure of this: I am with you always, even to the end of the age.

Matthew 28:18-20

It is clear from Scripture that reaching the unreached is the finish line for the church.

You are worthy to take the scroll and break its seals and open it. For you were slaughtered, and your blood has ransomed people for God from <u>every tribe and language and people and nation.</u>

Revelation 5:9

This is the target area that is most often neglected by churches. Years ago, it was an area in which I was also ignorant. As a local church we didn't feel that this was part of our calling. You may feel that same way. Who do you know that is engaging the unreached in these areas, and what could you do if you *did* know someone who was concerned about them?

Dr. Howard Foltz was my missions professor at Regent University. I had several required classes in missions with him, and he, along with others changed my perspective of reaching out to the unreached. He and others helped us strategically engage the area of the *ends of the earth*. As of this writing, our local church has been actively engaged in sponsoring and helping to train leaders in over 800 new church plants among the unreached, primarily in the 10/40 window. It required a target, a strategy, and a way to get involved. It wasn't as difficult as I thought it would be.

Later in this book, we will look further into how you may become part of this target area. For now, open your eyes and see the harvest among the unreached. It is possible your local church can be more effective among the unreached than it is, even within your local area. It is a privilege from God to be part of the *whole harvest* in Jerusalem, Judea, Samaria, and the ends of the earth.

To the early church Rome represented the ends of the earth. They were successful in penetrating even Caesar's household with the good news. *They were successful.* How much more can we in our day, with the internet, jet planes, cell phones, and satellites reach to the farthest corners of the earth. When we do, we will hasten the day of Jesus' return to the earth.

> ***...looking for and hastening the coming of the day of God***
> 2 Peter 3:12 NKJV

CHAPTER TEN

ENGAGING YOUR WORLD

NOW THAT ALL FOUR AREAS have been identified and it is clear that we are called in some way to all four simultaneously, how do we go about engaging in these areas? How can we strategically use our resources of time, money, talent, and attention to effectively engage all four areas?

After identifying your harvest field in light of Acts 1:8, the next step is to begin to engage the harvest. I needed some help in this area in order to be strategic. All missions activity is smart, but some missions activity is smarter. In other words, activity alone isn't always the answer. It is important to strategically engage.

After identifying the target, it is important to identify the barriers. We talked about these in an earlier chapter; some of the barriers are:

- The message is an offense to unbelievers.
- Different cultures, even within a single nation can keep real communication from happening.
- Geographical and language barriers can block the message.
- We could have an unclear or faulty interpretation of Scripture and the purpose of God.
- We face a fear of other nations and people groups.
- We must confront the very real barrier of spiritual warfare.

The curse of Babel must be overcome. A native is said to have told a missionary, "If God loves me so much, why doesn't he speak my language?"

It is important to be very specific about the obstacles faced in each target area believing that God has a way to crash through every one of them. This is the strategy we used as a church as we began to engage our world.

Pray for the world. Pray individually, corporately, and in special focused meetings. This is the most important part. Seeking God and his direction is the key to everything else. Binding the strong man in prayer and faith opens the door to ministry.

Learn and teach Biblical missions and God's view of people. Faith for the world comes as it is taught from Scripture. It takes some time for a church to accept a world vision. It will not come overnight, but is the result of intentional targeted teaching.

Expose the church to people of other cultures. Once people see that other cultures are just people who look and think differently, a love and respect for them can be cultivated. *Red and yellow, black and white, all are precious in his sight.*

Target all four areas with your finances. We tithe as a church to missions so it just makes sense to divide that tithe into four parts with each part designated to a different area. We give 25% of our tithe *as a minimum* to our Jerusalem and the same to our Judea, Samaria, and the ends of the earth.

Identify people in your tribe or group who are reaching into areas you have been neglecting. We didn't have people in our congregation who were reaching out to *the ends of the earth*, so we began partnering with those who were. God made some divine connections such as AIMS (Accelerating International Missions Strategies) and the CLUB1040.COM with Matt and Julie Beemer in the Middle East.

Give, go, and send as it says in Romans:

> **But how can they <u>call</u> on him to <u>save</u> them unless they <u>believe</u> in him? And how can they believe in him if they have never <u>heard</u> about him? And how can they hear about him unless someone <u>tells them</u>? ¹⁵ And how will anyone go and tell them without being <u>sent</u>? That is why the Scriptures say, "How beautiful are the feet of messengers who bring good news!"**
> Romans 10:14-15

Notice all of the action words in that passage of Scripture: call, save, believe, hear, tell (preach), and send. The take away is to start *acting.*

Begin the process, and believe the Lord will direct your steps in his plan for you and your church.

It is very important to see engaging the world as a process. It isn't reasonable to change or add everything at once. Start with *Jerusalem*. Are you reaching the people closest to you now? A plane ride overseas isn't enough to make you effective if you aren't doing it now.

As you examine where you are now, you may already be doing some of it, although you may not have identified it properly. Now is the time to take steps towards full engagement. Adding the areas that have been neglected is a process, and making necessary changes could take a year or two.

In our case, the area that was completely neglected was reaching the ends of the earth. We didn't see the call for us personally for years, and even after we did we didn't know how to begin. God put us in partnership with those who were already doing it well, so we became more focused over time. The important thing is to get in traffic so God can direct you. As someone said, it is hard to steer a parked car. It is amazing how the Holy Spirit is attracted to *movement*. Begin in faith and he will lead you. Divine connections show up once we are open to them. There are probably some very good opportunities close to you already. The future is exciting to those who are following God in the area where his heart is: people.

There are many effective ways to engage each of the four areas of outreach. We have had success with some and others didn't work as well, but we never stopped trying. Each area has its unique methods of evangelism and outreach.

- Jerusalem: We primarily use relational evangelism where Christians befriend someone away from God, and develop a relationship with them. Someone said you don't win your enemies to the Lord, just your friends. At the right time, you may have an opportunity to share your story and Jesus' story. You may just invite them to attend church or an event with you.

- Judea: This can take many avenues. We started a campus fifteen miles from us. We also are involved with Significant Church Network where we reach out to pastors in small town and small county America to encourage them. You may plant churches, campuses, or support others who reach your region.

- Samaria: In many cases your Samaria is far from you geographically. Outreach in this area can be prayer, supporting missionaries, short-term missions trips from your church to these regions, and many other ways. I tend to think of this area as a foreign culture or nation. Usually it has been reached some with the message of Jesus. Europe fits this category to us. Instead of calling Europe reached, it is now being called *formerly* reached.

- Ends of the Earth: This is usually the area that we let drop. I encourage you to start the process. Pray and ask God to lead you to a partner. Check your denomination or group and see who is reaching out now to the unreached. When you connect with a partner, support them with finances and encouragement. Your church, or a group of like-minded churches may want to consider adopting an unreached people group. We can help you do this through AIMS.

We made mistakes along the way and the process took longer than we expected. The price we pay to reach people will be well worth it when we see people in heaven from every tribe and tongue that may be there simply because of our willingness to obey God.

CHAPTER ELEVEN

RECEIVING GOD'S POWER FOR MISSIONS

YOU CAN'T DO THIS ALONE. God never intended you to. Acts 1:8 is very clear about God's intention to empower his people to reach out. Imagine being one of the eleven remaining disciples when Jesus told them his expectations of them. They were to take his message to the entire world so that everyone could hear. Do you think they felt overwhelmed? I certainly would have, and still do, except for his Acts 1:8 promise:

> *But you will receive power when the Holy Spirit comes upon you. And you will be my witnesses, telling people about me everywhere—in Jerusalem, throughout Judea, in Samaria, and to the ends of the earth.*

It is impossible to overstate the place of God's power in missions. Jesus Christ's message was accompanied by power encounters. He regularly cast out demons and healed the sick.

The early church continued in this power with healings and miracles. There never was an *age of miracles*; there is a *God of miracles*. He confirms his message with accompanying signs, wonders, and miracles.

The wisdom of men empties the cross of its power according to the Apostle Paul writing to the Corinthians (1 Corinthians 1:17-2:5). We see Paul and the rest of the early church regularly exercising and walking in the power of the Spirit of God.

It is often discussed why it seems miracles occur in other cultures during mass evangelistic meetings more than in the Western church. The answer in Scripture is: power accompanies the *movement* of the message. When we see in Scripture and in our times a great manifestation of power it is almost always accompanying the message into new territory. Power evangelism is a message that can be seen and heard.

> *Yet I dare not boast about anything except what Christ has done through me, bringing the Gentiles to God by my message and by the way I worked among them. They were convinced by the power of miraculous signs and wonders and by the power of God's Spirit. In this way, I have fully presented the Good News of Christ from Jerusalem all the way to Illyricum. My ambition has always been to preach the Good News where the name of Christ has never been heard, rather than where a church has already been started by someone else.*
> Romans 15:18-20

Paul makes it clear that the gospel is only fully presented when it can be seen and heard. Often the Western church has tried to intellectually present the gospel, however, the wisdom of men empties the cross of its power. Jesus and the early church knew the futility of an intellectual gospel alone.

T.L. Osborn was a very effective missionary evangelist around the world in the 20th century. As a young man he and his wife Daisy journeyed to India to reach the lost. He told about setting his black book next to a Muslim's black book and trying to convince him that Jesus was the Messiah and Savior. It didn't work. They came home where he had a powerful encounter with the risen Lord. Later, they returned to India and many other places and preached a very simple gospel accompanied with miracles and healings. It worked this time. He and Daisy reached millions of people worldwide and inspired a new generation to believe God for his power gifts to follow the message.

Mark Noll makes an amazing assessment of the effects of power in world missions:

"One of the most momentous developments in the recent history of Christianity must certainly be the emergence of Pentecostalism as a dynamic force around the world. In 1900 there were, at most, a bare handful of Christians who were experiencing special gifts of the Holy Spirit similar to those recorded in the New Testament. By the year 2010, as many as 600 million (or more than a quarter of the worldwide population of Christian adherents) could be identified as Pentecostal or Charismatic. Pentecostal and charismatic currents have been central in the rapid expansion of Christianity outside of the west, with most of the rapidly growing churches in Brazil, Nigeria, Korea, Russia, China, and many

other nations. In these situations, Pentecostal and charismatic forms of Christian faith flourish by directly confronting pagan gods and animistic spirits as well as by imparting the direct immediacy of God's presence. Should recent trends continue with Pentecostal and charismatic forces continuing to expand, especially in the Majority World, events around 1900 that precipitated identifiable Christians movements defined by belief in the special work of the Holy Spirit will continue to loom as one of the most decisive turning points in the recent history of Christianity." [12]

Another important aspect of receiving God's power for missions is to believe you are personally empowered *wherever you live.* One of the unfortunate misconceptions in world missions is that it is the job of the Western church to reach the nations. Jesus clearly says: *you* shall receive power. This applies to Christians in every part of the world. Why would the Great Commission only apply to the Western Church? God trusts you to follow him, be a witness, and empower others to do the same. The Great Commission belongs to every Christian, everywhere.

If you are in a developing nation, he will give your church the resources and opportunities to reach those beyond, the same as he has for the American church. The church in every nation is important and empowered to be a witness to the entire world.

The key to the power Jesus promised, is to keep it moving. *Movement of the message and power go together.* Expect supernatural help as you focus on God's target: the whole world.

CHAPTER TWELVE

STOP STARING INTO HEAVEN

So when the apostles were with Jesus, they kept asking him, "Lord, has the time come for you to free Israel and restore our kingdom?"

He replied, "The Father alone has the authority to set those dates and times, and they are not for you to know. But you will receive power when the Holy Spirit comes upon you. And you will be my witnesses, telling people about me everywhere—in Jerusalem, throughout Judea, in Samaria, and to the ends of the earth."

After saying this, he was taken up into a cloud while they were watching, and they could no longer see him. As they strained to see him rising into heaven, two white-robed men suddenly stood among them. "Men of Galilee," they said, "why are you standing here staring into heaven? Jesus has been taken from you into heaven, but someday

he will return from heaven in the same way you saw him go!
Acts 1:6-11

T HE ANGELS ASKED why the disciples were just standing there staring into heaven when Jesus had just told them what to do and where to do it. Often that can be our response to Jesus' instructions as well. God is attracted to *movement*. The book of Acts is a story of movement.

The angels were saying "get moving." Like the disciples, we can be so focused on what is going to *happen next* that we forget what we should *do next*. Someone called that syndrome the paralysis of analysis. Prayerful planning is great but it should lead to action.

The angels made it clear that Jesus would return in the same way he left. Rather than trying to figure out who the antichrist is or if Jupiter will align with Mars, *start moving*. It may lead to a movement.

The book of Acts is the story of the early church from its beginning in Jerusalem on the day of Pentecost, to the culmination of Paul's ministry in the capital of the empire, Rome. We have since that time benefited greatly from the examples left to us by the focused and fired up early church.

Not only is the Book of Acts a story and a history of the early church, it is a strategy that we can follow in the 21st century to do it again. They effectively reached Rome and its empire. Jesus gave them a simple message and power that accompanied it. By that strategy they targeted those who had not yet heard; man and God working together reached a lost world.

Our challenge is to not just *see* what was accomplished, but *how* it was accomplished. By diligently seeking God and letting him bring expression to our efforts, we can reach all nations in this generation.

I sometimes feel what those early church disciples must have felt, overwhelmed. But they accepted the challenge and so should we. With God all things are possible. Our destiny is to say *yes* to God and boldly go into the world that doesn't know God and in some cases is resistant to him. Jesus said the very gates of hell could not resist the church he is building.

The purpose of this book is to encourage and inspire local churches and pastors around the world to look beyond their four walls and even their communities, to the regions beyond. God said if we asked him he would give the nations as our inheritance and the ends of the earth as our possession. (Psalm 2:8)

AIMS (Accelerating International Missions Strategies) can assist you in taking the next step towards mobilizing to reach *the ends of the earth*. It offers seminars and materials to get you started. The website is: www.aims.org

I am also personally available to discuss with local church leaders how they may become more engaged in reaching all four areas of Acts 1:8. My email is terry@fcfc.tv and my church website is www.fcfc.tv .

Just as Jesus expanded the vision of the early disciples in Acts 1 to look beyond their nation to the entire world, may we ask him to help us focus on the whole world as well. Ask him, he will show you what to do next.

Appendix

ATTRIBUTES OF A MISSIONS MOBILIZED CHURCH

The following material is adapted from the AIMS publication *On the Cutting Edge*.
www.AIMS.org

Directions For Using the *Twenty Attributes* Check List

THIS CHECKLIST HAS BEEN DESIGNED from the AIMS experience of mobilizing local churches for world missions over the past 30 years. If you will take this quick *mission check-up* quiz, it will help you evaluate the current missions status (activity) of your church. The mobilization process will vary depending on the size, financial base, leadership style, etc., of each church. The AIMS publication titled *On The Cutting Edge* is an effective tool for a church to use in evaluating and planning its own program. We encourage you and your church to adopt and move towards fulfilling the six measurable criteria of a *missions mobilized church*:

Praying Giving Ministering Sending Assisting Cooperating

The following are some guidelines for taking the check-up:

1. Read each statement, and respond by filling in the most appropriate number for your church. Don't think too long, the first number that comes to your mind is probably the best one.

2. Add up your total and put the score in the space at the bottom of the page.

3. **There is not a *pass* or *fail* score for this check-up.** The only way that any church can fail is to not obey God when He speaks about mobilizing further.

4. Later, you can have your elders, deacons or missions committee do this check-up together. Then, they can compare their scores and use this as a means for discussion.

5. The twenty attributes are not arranged in any particular order of priority. In your thoughtful meditation and discussion, prioritize them yourself according to the need of your particular church. List the most important things for your church to begin improving on first, second, etc.

May God richly bless you as you prayerfully consider the application of this check-up to your church's missions outreach.

Twenty Attributes of a Missions Mobilized Church

The criteria for a *Great Commission Church* are listed below.

Mark a number 0 through 5 for each attribute below (0 = no activity, 5 = full involvement), then total the score:

_____ 1.   Teaching on missions in Sunday School, sermons, missions newsletter, home cells, etc.

_____ 2.   Regular intercessory prayer for the lost world, focusing on the unreached.

_____ 3.   Missions team or fellowship group which meets at least monthly.

_____ 4.   Church hosts regular missions conferences.

_____ 5.   Systematic financial involvement of congregation for missions.

_____ 6.   A focus on praise and worship that expresses the missionary heart of God and inspires the congregation to missions involvement.

_____ 7.   Pastoral care for missionaries, with letters, phone calls, gifts, visits, email, etc.

_____ 8.   Has a missions secretary or pastor/director.

_____ 9.   Goals, objectives, and policies defined for mission program.

_____ 10.   Local cross-cultural outreach.

_____ 11. Missions projects, such as church building or equipment purchasing.

_____ 12. Missions-minded pastor who travels to a mission field regularly.

_____ 13. Short-term outreaches for congregation's members and staff.

_____ 14. Identification and training of missionary candidates within the congregation.

_____ 15. Career or *tentmaker* missionaries sent out and supported by the church.

_____ 16. Program to reproduce and share your missions vision with other churches.

_____ 17. *Adoption* of (or preparing to adopt) an unreached people group.

_____ 18. Regular missionary guests.

_____ 19. The entire church *knows* the missionaries, not just the pastors and church staff.

_____ 20. Vision of local church as a *missions base*.

_____**Total**

Endnotes

Chapter 1

[1] C. Peter Wagner. *The Book of Acts*. Regal. 2008. Page 220-221.

[2] Gordon D. Fee and Douglas Stuart. *How to Read the Bible for All it's Worth*. Zondervan Publishing House. 1993. Page 98

[3] C. Peter Wagner. *The Book of Acts*. Regal. 2008. Page 15.

Chapter 2

[4] Gangel, K.O. (1998). *Holman New Testament Commentary, Acts* (Vol. 5, p.27). Nashville, TN: Broadman & Holman Publishers.

[5] https://www.biblegateway.com/resources/ivp-nt/Miracles-Effect

Chapter 3

[6] https://enduringword.com/commentary/acts-8

Chapter 9

[7] https://gotquestions.org/Samaritans.html

[8] http://www.brainyquote.com/quotes/quotes/m/martinluth297520.html

[9] https://joshuaproject.net/resources/articles/has_everyone_heard

[10] Strong, J. (2009). *A Concise Dictionary of the Words in the Greek Testament and The Hebrew Bible* (Vol. 2, p. 74). Bellingham, WA: Logos Bible Software.

[11] Zodhiates, S. (2000). *The Complete Word Study Dictionary: New Testament* (electronic ed.). Chattanooga, TN: AMG Publishers.

Chapter 11

[12] Mark Noll, *Turning Points: Decisive Moments in the History of Christianity* (Grand Rapids: Baker, 2012), 310-313

About the Author

TERRY LEE ROBERTS, along with his wife Rebecca, have been pastors at Faith Christian Family Church in Warrenton, Missouri, USA, for over three decades. In addition to pastoring a church with a heart for the world, they have made over 40 short-term-missions trips. Terry served first as an assistant pastor in Glasgow, Scotland before returning to the mid-western United States where he and Rebecca grew up. He is a graduate of Rhema Bible Training College, Fontbonne University and Regent University. Terry is currently working on his doctorate at Asbury Theological Seminary.

Serving as the Vice-President of AIMS (Accelerating International Missions Strategies) in Colorado Springs, Colorado, has further fueled his passion for reaching the nations for Jesus Christ. Preaching, and teaching leadership principles to those serving God has taken him to many European and eastern European nations.

Terry and his wife, Rebecca, reside in Wentzville, Missouri. Their family includes Jessica, her husband Jeremiah; Jonathan, his wife Nicole, and their grandsons Oliver and Finnian.

Terry may be reached at terry@fcfc.tv or the website at www.fcfc.tv

Terry Roberts shares an introduction to
Christian doctrine and practice.

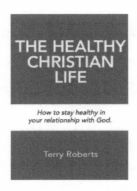

Coming Soon: Heaven is an exciting discussion of
the coming eternity in heaven.

Now available in paperback and Kindle at Amazon.com

Made in the USA
Middletown, DE
26 May 2021